VIOLET

Books by Selima Hill

Saying Hello at the Station (Chatto & Windus, 1984)*

My Darling Camel (Chatto & Windus, 1988)*

The Accumulation of Small Acts of Kindness (Chatto & Windus, 1989)

A Little Book of Meat (Bloodaxe Books, 1993)

Trembling Hearts in the Bodies of Dogs: New & Selected Poems
(Bloodaxe Books, 1994): includes work from titles asterisked above,
and the complete text of *The Accumulation of Small Acts of Kindness*

Violet (Bloodaxe Books, 1997)

SELIMA HILL

Violet

BLOODAXE BOOKS

ISBN: 1 85224 400 3

First published 1997 by
Bloodaxe Books Ltd,
P.O. Box 1SN,
Newcastle upon Tyne NE99 1SN.

Bloodaxe Books Ltd acknowledges
the financial assistance of Northern Arts.

Cover printing by J. Thomson Colour Printers Ltd, Glasgow.

Printed in Great Britain by
Cromwell Press Ltd, Broughton Gifford, Melksham, Wiltshire.

*'To get to the poetic truth it is
not always necessary to tell the
what-actually-happened truth;
these times I lie.'*

RITA ANN HIGGINS

Acknowledgements

MY SISTER'S SISTER

My Sister's Sister was one of the winners of the Poetry Business Competition in 1995, and was published as a pamphlet by Smith/ Doorstop Books in 1996 under the title *My Sister's Horse*. Some of the poems also appeared in *As Girls Can Boast* (Oscars Press, 1994), *London Magazine* and *The Rialto*.

MY HUSBAND'S WIFE

Acknowledgements are due to the editors of the following publications in which some of these poems, or earlier versions of them, first appeared: *Heat* (New Zealand), *London Magazine, Mind Readings* (Minerva, 1996), *The North, Poetry Review, Poetry Wales* and *Sycamore* (Indiana). 'Being a Grandmother' was commissioned by *Bookworm* (BBC-1 Television) and 'Please Can I Have a Man' by BBC World Service. Some of these poems were broadcast on *Stanza* (BBC Radio 4), and 'Please Can I Have a Man' was broadcast on *Pick of the Week* (BBC Radio 4).

Contents

MY SISTER'S SISTER

My Sister's Tooth

I watch for her until she's really there,
crossing open fields strewn with limbs
she has to pick her way through very carefully
in order to get safely home to me –
me, a little girl in yellow shorts
waiting for the tooth she promised me,
a human tooth embedded in a bean
and carved into the shape of a poodle.

My Sister's Nose

Everybody marvels at her nose.
It's beautiful and slender, like her mother's.
I, her younger sister, marvel at
the way she talks to men I do not know.

My Sister's Kitten

Our mother likes to feed me perfect veal;
and two invisible drops of Radiostol
are wobbled on my morning toast by Nurse –
a special little wafer, like a host.
She feeds my upstairs sister next to nothing.
At least, that's what my upstairs sister thinks.
And when I try to move her head I can't.
And when her little kitten starts to lick her,
bit by bit, as if she were a skyscraper
a tiny Tippex brush is painting white,
I run into the yard to greet the wasps,
and let the licking carry on all night –
my sister on her bed, and me outside,
my naked body smeared with marmalade.

My Sister and I Visit the Zoo

My sister kindly takes me to the zoo
where very soon I get completely lost
and spend the day waiting in LOST CHILDREN
until my sister comes at closing time,
neither of us having seen the animals
whose smells like buns I carry carefully home.

My Sister and I Go on Holiday

A spotted dog is struggling to give birth
and someone in a lacy shawl is waving
but, hidden in our hats, we hurry on,
not forgetting, in her hand, the knife
our doctor has insisted we take with us.

My Sister's Hats

She stands beside their open cars at night
posing like a llama in a hat –
sometimes white like felted piano keys,
sometimes crinkly green and blue like money.

What Does My Sister Do Behind Her Door?

She catches angry wasps in blue glass jars,
she stows a sum of money in an owl,
she slides a folder underneath her bed,
breeds unwanted kittens, ripens plums;
she thinks about her sister hiding somewhere
scribbling in her notebook like a spy,
she thinks *she thinks she loves me but she doesn't,*
she doesn't understand a word I say;
she waits until the cars have driven off
then quickly gets undressed and goes downstairs.

My Sister Goes to Italy

My sister can't decide which to choose.
First one, and then the other, take her out.
Finally the problem is solved:
she gets engaged to both of them at once.
When little Bee and six-foot Boo find out,
my mother puts a notice in *The Times*,
packs her bags, and takes her off to Italy –
leaving me to feed the seven kittens,
and sex them with my finger in their fur.

My Sister Has Twins

The twins are sleeping soundly
in the nursery
while out beyond the car park
in the sun
their mother
in a nightie and a duffle coat
is catching
the first bus to the sea.

My Sister's Poodle Is Accused of Eating the Housekeeping Money

Everybody's standing in the kitchen
staring at a normal-looking dog
that actually, according to my sister,
contains the missing twenty five-pound-notes.
We stare at it some more.
It doesn't move,
taking neither one side nor the other.

My Sister Says She Wants to Play the Piano

The trouble is she has to be alone,
so here we are, trooping round the fields,
dressed in aprons, towels, indoor slippers,
pretending we can hear determined practising;
in the dappled drawing-room, meanwhile,
the piano sleeps as soundly as a fish
dreaming of the day it rolls over
and floats away indifferently downstream.

My Sister's Dress

Down she comes,
her hair a strange yellow,
her little dress so tight
she can't sit down.
But where does she go to?
And why does she go for so long?
Nobody knows,
and nobody wants to know.
Perhaps a storm has swept the bridge away,
perhaps she's sick,
perhaps obeying orders –
stealing carp,
mutilating horses,
running baths
for lonely heiresses.
But do we ask her
in the morning?
No. Everyone just stares at her,
like idiots,
as, half asleep, she floats
across the lawn
in clouds of lace
and minuscule high heels.

My Sister on My Wedding Day

She slips into the bathroom during breakfast
and nothing will induce her to come out
till finally I have to dress downstairs.
Actually I like it. We all do.
We like her being locked in a room
softening and warming herself.

My Sister and I Have Breakfast

She spoons the fruit between her teeth like jewels,
cube by peeled cube – trickling juice,
and letting the long sleeves of her nightdress
fill the air with time like a vat
round and round whose brittle rim the ambulance
calls the faithful to their red ice-cream.

My Sister and I Finally Arrive at the Hospital

She sweeps onto the ward like a bride
with armfuls of white nighties and fresh flowers
that beam *Come on.* My sister beams *Get back.*
You mustn't touch. You mustn't speak to her.
Or even look as if you're able to.
You have to stand where I can see you, Darling,
but not too close. And never say a word.
But, very quickly, once, I risk a whisper.
My mother whispers back. We both agree
it won't be long before she dies. However
my sister must be humoured till she does.

My Sister Leans Over the Bed

When I see her take your hand like that
something heavy like an unwashed fish
rises to the surface of my skin
and drags itself about, as if it's lonely.
Mother – I'm not thinking of you.
I'm thinking of the safety of the Ladies.
Of standing by the sinks with nothing on
and refusing to open the door until I'm clean.

My Sister and I in the Lift

Every day I dread stepping out.
I dread the ward. I dread the corridor.
I dread the sight of seeing her in bed.
I dread the rush of sweat inside my clothes.
I dread the hours of having to be brave.
But failing to be brave would be much worse.
Or maybe failing's being braver still.
Can everybody please leave the ward.
I want to be alone with my mother.
They lost her in the bowels of the hospital.
She waited in her wheelchair all day.
My sister must be bodily removed.
Injected with a sedative if necessary.
The two of us are sisters it is true
but have you noticed how we never speak?
We used to have a doll called Violet
that used to smell of violet cachous.
Or did I just imagine it? The kisses?
Did I just imagine those as well?
Give us back the bald velvet face
stuffed with straw that creaked
when we cuddled her, give us back
the cheeks we kissed to shreds,
so we can learn tenderness again.
Please remove all the other patients,
or let them die, if they want to, too.
Bring them wild flowers. Nothing else.
Listen to them. Listen to them. Listen to them.

My Sister's Doll

She dresses her in dresses like a doll,
and tries her out in different positions,
as if she's still alive, which she's not,
or barely is, or won't be by tomorrow:
but still she tries to prop her up and feed her,
to think it won't be long before she's home,
before she's reunited with her horses,
before we hear the thundering of hooves,
the roads crack open, hospitals collapse,
and beds emerge in hundreds from the ruins
to flap and honk their way across the sky.

My Sister's Secret Rule

My sister has a secret rule: *pretend.*
Pretend we are two normal human beings.
Pretend we are too well-brought-up to lie.
Pretend our mother's feeling *twice the person.*
Pretend we are not lost. But we are.
The falling snow may smell of violets
but it is falling snow nonetheless.

My Sister's Horse

She drives until she can't drive any more.
And then she drives some more. And then she stops.
She thinks she can't be seen but she can.
I'm watching her reflection in the mirror.
It slips into a shop and buys a paper
and reads it in a corner like a thief.
Then hides it in a box of tennis balls.
But why is she so secretive about it?
And why does she keep asking me for cash?
And why do I keep saying *Yes of course*
and why can't people look her in the eye?
And why can't I? And where are all my friends?
And why can't they be told our mother died?
She died this afternoon like a lamb.
We left her covered up on her bed,
took away her things in a bag,
and tipped the flowers into a litter bin.
My sister's gone all tall like a nail.
The mirror's playing tricks on us, I see.
Now she reappears as my sister,
slides a tub of ice-cream on my lap,
changes back into her driving shoes
and drives away as fast as she can.

My Sister and I Meet on the Stairs

She comes up very close,
then turns away,
and, as she turns, she whispers *You killed her*
before retiring stiffly to her room
as if she never said or thought anything.

My Sister's Sister

Every night before I went to sleep
I wrote about our day at the hospital,
and what I hoped, and what I feared, and why;
I wrote about the flowers by her bed,
her cards, her pills, her weight, her temperature,
everything, in fact, except my sister,
or anything connected with my sister.
I do not want her in my private books
where everything exists because of me.
I do not want her rootling around
as if she has to stay because she's true.

The Night My Mother Died I Dreamt of Sailors

I dreamt of sailors sailing past an island
and being startled by the sound of paws
scraping inconsolably on concrete
as animals that used to live in luxury
in special villas cooled by giant flowers
find themselves abandoned by their keepers
and having to survive on dry roots.

My Sister's Horse

She gazes at her body in the mirror,
then gets undressed, and gazes again;
she feasts her little arms on chilly lotion
that wriggles in her palm like chocolate crème;
she plucks her fuzz, she dusts her crevices,
she sucks her razored shins' vermilion nicks;
she seals letters, doctors photographs,
slithers hairless kittens down her bed,
she sniffs her cache of violet cachous
and scans the sky for signs of airborne men;
she feels envy, like a swimming pool,
its room-sized weight, weighing down her room;
and as she falls asleep she hears a racehorse
breathing in the dark outside her door,
the hole that someone's cut into its neck
expanding and contracting as it breathes.

My Sister and I Go Shopping

I offer, first of all, of course, to pay.
To give my name. My sister's. To explain.
To do whatever I have to to get out,
to soften the heart of the man
who grips her arm,
crêpey now and grey like wrinkled stockings,
that used to peek out
from the puffed sleeves
of her pink angora cardigan
so sweetly
long ago –
before she changed,
before it got so cold,
before we got involved in this stupid funeral.

My Sister and the Vicar

Absolutely not
the vicar says,
drawing on the only cigarette
ever smoked inside our mother's house.
My sister understands.
The vicar smiles,
moving on to chocolate-coated cakes.
But on the very morning of the funeral,
she bicycles alone to the village
and, with the help of two confused fishermen,
moves the altar back to where it was.
Back to where it was, like a ship
on its way to where the world ends.

My Sister's Jeans

My sixty-year-old 'forty-year-old' sister,
whose head I dream of floating muslin over,
acres of it, drenched in chloroform,
comes teetering down from the bathroom
in clouds of talc
where what she has done she has
squeezed herself into some shorts
so shockingly short they extrude her like polystyrene,
gleaming, insistent, discoloured, and up to no good,
and reeking of something,
and stuffed full of something alive,
of eyeballs, ferrets, cheeses, swelling hymns,
that she could no more come and sit down beside me in,
no more sit down anywhere in,
and become my sister again,
than a beautiful woman,
whose naked and suckable nipples probe the air
can shimmy up against a wall of mouths
and not be unstable.

My Sister Wants a Muff

My sister wants a muff,
a Persian cat,
a peach, a pool,
a white jardinière;
she wants a little car
to run around in,
a moor, a gun, a lover, HRT,
but most of all she wants my late father –
the way a chandelier would a cosh:
to smash itself to bits with late at night
when everybody else is making love
at lots of deeply satisfying angles.

My Sister's Shoes

Why are her shoes so tight and uncomfortable-looking?
Why are her eyes so big and her waist so small?
Where are her dogs, and why are they all chained up?
Who was she with, and why was he holding a gun?
Who is her father, and why is he never around?
And what does she want? And why is she dressed like that?
And who does she scream at? And why does she scream at me?
And what do I feel? And what do I think?
Estranged.
My sister and myself are *estranged.*
We sit apart and sulk like skinny vultures
growing old together in one cage.

My Sister Loses Her Temper
in a Room Full of Children

The children hold their dolls and watch me cry.
And then I feel my daughter take my hand
and lead me up to bed,
to counting sheep,
to dreaming in the little painted bed
the children are still playing with downstairs.

My Sister Calls Me Darling

It isn't really me
she calls Darling
but another, better, sister
she's invented
who lies and steals
and takes our mother fishing
and shakes her senseless
by the gleaming lake –
vicious daughters
red of lip and hair
who top her up and top her up with morphine.

My Sister's Head

You can't come in, it says.
There's been an accident.
So back I trot,
past the famous roses,
past the gate,
past the sign we painted –
directing neither no one to no accident
nor me to what I've got to learn's not home.

My Sister Has Visitors

When the men from the city,
weighed down by documents and unsuitable clothes,
finally arrive,
my sister hands round various improvised bats
and herds them into the barn to play pingpong
till one by one they sink into the straw
where cows with squints force tongues inside their ears.

The Meeting

When we met that evening on the stairs,
the evening of the day our mother died,
she looked at me as if she didn't know me,
as if she was already out of reach,
someone years of pain had made untouchable,
had dipped in glass for their own good.

My Sister Goes to London for the Day

The only sign of life is one old dog,
black and white, chained to the gate.
Someone he once knew when he was young
unclips the chain and puts him in a van
and takes him to a new, and kinder, home.
Or does he think his owner will come back,
the one he used to have, before the chain,
and, finding him no longer at the gate,
does he think he hears her calling him?
And in the evening, when he doesn't come,
does she leave a door slightly open
before advancing with a shrimping net
alone across the heath to catch him hares?

Giant Cows

It's in a dream but they don't know it yet.
Sunlight bathes the children on the lawn.
Everyone is dressed in white and laughing.
The giant cows are paddling in the stream.
Smell the lilac. Smell the famous roses.
It's in a dream. The dream has got it wrong.
I look at her and realise she's the one.
I have to go immediately. *Forgive me.*
Afraid, polite, my mother will obey.
She does not know that childhood is over.
She does not know my sister is the one
I want to be contained until she's still,
I want to be absolved, like a moth,
I want to be absolved and pacified,
softened, crumbled, charred and turned to powder,
I want to say *it's over* to, and touch;
but in the dream it's only just begun.
It looks as if it's perfect but it's not.
I watch them as they laugh and drink their tea
as if they're Them, like That, and never won't be –
and walk away, unable to explain
the day's a dream but they don't know it yet.

My Sister's Christian Name and the Word Darling

Certain words I know I shouldn't use.
Fucked-up liar. Crêpey. HRT.
I know I shouldn't. But I sometimes do.
Other words I ought to use I can't.
I grab at them and whack them on the head.
Otherwise I know I can't think straight.

I Am Hers and She Is Mine

When I was young I knitted flocks of sheep.
I kept them like an army on the landing,
drilled to watch her door, and storm her room,
reporting back on everything they saw.
And in the winter as the days drew in
I knitted every sheep a little cardigan
to keep them warm at night while they waited.
They waited. But she never came back.
She went away to be a grown woman.
Our partnership however gathered strength.
We spent our lives perfecting being enemies
and now it's automatic: I am hers
and she – whom now I only meet in dreams,
with painted face and dogs on chains – is mine.

MY HUSBAND'S WIFE

Why I Left You

When you had quite finished
dragging me across your bed
like a band of swaggering late-night removal men
dragging a piano
the size and shape of the United States of America
across a tent,
I left the room,
and slipped into the garden,
where I gulped down whole mouthfuls of delicious aeroplanes
that taxied down my throat
still wrapped in sky
with rows of naked women in their bellies
telling me to go,
and I went,
and that's why I did it,
and everything told me so –
tracks that I knew the meaning of
like the tracks of a wolf
wolf-hunters know the exact colour of
by the tracks of the tracks alone.
You get a feeling for it.
You stand in the garden at night
with blood getting crisp on your thighs
and feel the stars spiralling right down
out of the sky into your ears,
burrowing down inside your ears
like drip-fed needles
saying *Get out. Now.*
By 'you' I mean me.
One of us had to:
I did.

Those Little Fish

Those little lop-sided fish
that ply gravely up and down
the tiny oceans of propelling-pencils
dreaming of the day
they're called upon to deliver speeches
to hundreds and thousands of wide-eyed
propelling-pencil manufacturers
clinging to rafts,
speeches that are almost impossible to make out
because the waves are so big,
and their mouths are full of water,
and they're facing the wrong way,
and anyway they only speak in
fish language,
those little fish –
OK they're dumb –
can be encouraged;
but you,
even though I lay awake beside you
on rumpled coats
night after night
willing you to make
some little sign, some little squeak,
to squeak back to,
to be understanding of,
to apply my battery of dictionaries
and manuals and tracking devices
and calibrated sensors to,
don't even dream
that you speak.

Please Can I Have a Man

Please can I have a man who wears corduroy.
Please can I have a man
who knows the names of 100 different roses;
who doesn't mind my absent-minded rabbits
wandering in and out
as if they own the place,
who makes me creamy curries from fresh lemon-grass,
who walks like Belmondo in *A Bout de Souffle*;
who sticks all my carefully-selected postcards –
sent from exotic cities
he doesn't expect to come with me to,
but would if I asked, which I will do –
with nobody else's, up on his bedroom wall,
starting with Ivy, the Famous Diving Pig,
whose picture, in action, I bought ten copies of;
who talks like Belmondo too, with lips as smooth
and tightly-packed as chocolate-coated
(*melting* chocolate) peony buds;
who knows that piling himself stubbornly on top of me
like a duvet stuffed with library books and shopping-bags
is all too easy: please can I have a man
who is not prepared to do that.
Who is not prepared to say I'm 'pretty' either.
Who, when I come trotting in from the bathroom
like a squealing freshly-scrubbed piglet
that likes nothing better than a binge
of being affectionate and undisciplined and uncomplicated,
opens his arms like a trough for me to dive into.

Buckets

I came home from work
to find my kitchen had been completely taken over
by two strangers
who had decided to use it
as a field hospital,
and one was the wound
and one was the wounded patient,
and I was to be the orderly, apparently,
shifty-looking,
wearing enormous shoes,
who used to live with finches
like a finch,
whose kitchen
was a finches' wonderland;
who drags her mop around the coughed-up blood
clattering buckets
like a complete idiot.
And she is the blood
and you are the blood-stained patient
who's coughed her up
in the flightpaths of my joy.

Being Fifty

Being fifty makes me feel large,
large and cold
like someone else's fridge.
I harbour scarlet fish
and fat gold eggs
that men in suits
with hands like vets'
remove.
I never speak.
Sometimes I might hum.
Or very rarely
raise a strangled gurgle
as if I'm trying one last time to lurch forward,
to get my fluff-clogged ankles
free from the lino,
hone myself, develop a fluked tail,
acquire a taste for frogbit,
and push off –
paddle off across the world's wide oceans
like a flat-footed sofa
that's suddenly learnt how to swim,
piled high with jellies, cheeses, cushions,
fishes, poodles, babies, balding men,
swimming-pools, airing-cupboards, hospitals,
and tiny pills, like polystyrene granules,
people advise one, or not,
to start taking.

Your Girlfriend's Thigh

I've got what feels like a cross between
a family saloon car and an eel
the size and texture
of your girlfriend's thigh
lodged inside my stomach day and night
and what I want for my birthday is an avenue
wrapped in gold and silver and so long
the trees, let them be poplars, turn to dots
for me to watch her disappearing down.

How to Kill a Wolf

Being a wife is being good like me.
She doesn't lodge herself
in other people's ears
and grow and grow her dead-straight
headless stalks until your skull's
so full of yellow crops you keel over.
A wolf can get a seed in its ear
and die within a week:
it keels over.
She's like a seed.
Her polished hair's the sort
for slipping into hotel dining-rooms for dinner in
– dead straight.
She's slipped inside.
I am observing her.
She goes about her business like Van Gogh.
If anyone stopped her now
she'd cut their head off.
Do you know that?
It's like he said.
It's like a bad dream.
She's only happy when she's short of time.
If you say a word about the future
she'll gag you with her sulphurated veil.

The Fish Hospital

It's all very well you
shouting at me like that
and trying to get me to answer
your endless questions
but what you don't seem to realise is
that my head —
just as I thought it couldn't be
stretched so tight,
and feel so cold,
and creak like ice,
one minute longer —
has turned itself
into a goldfish-bowl
I have to use all my powers of concentration
to keep balanced,
and keep quiet,
for the sake of the fish
that squirm about at the bottom
in not enough water
like lips and tongues
being buried alive under snow,
that are struggling to cry,
but they can't,
they're not formed properly,
while outside in the fields
windswept nurses,
standing in the snow
in their dressing-gowns,
have finally given up waving
they're so cold.

Jesu's Blood

I've sawed it through the throat with a carving-knife –
I'm talking about my platinum ex-wedding ring –
I've made it sharp and jagged like a star
minnows and pixies would use –
you wouldn't get that –
the colour of heart-broken nights
and spinach-leaf veins.
I'm trying not to send it back. I won't.
I won't be angry. Can you understand that?
I see my job as making people happy –
writing little cards and wrapping gifts
in twists of sugared-almond-coloured wrapping-paper.
Wrap it up in Jesu's blood more like.
You can't buy Jesu's blood at Debenhams.
Debenhams is where ex-husbands go
to furnish their ex-wives' exhumed ex-bedrooms.

Red Cows

I remember the day we got married.
Very nice.
Prettiness was all I thought about.
It never entered my head to think about *you*.
Who were you?
Were you there?
I can't think why.
I must have told you *Marry*
and you married.
I must have told you
spend the whole week crying.
I gave you food
you didn't know how to eat.
I gave you tears
you didn't know how to shed.
I gave you the moon
like a cold disc on our bed.
We journeyed on,
two white and lonely ships
shifting our consignments
through dull oceans
only crossed
by those who had lost their minds,
who dreamed they sighted herring-gulls
and coconuts;
who when they woke,
a million miles from anywhere,
saw herds of red cows
running down a mountainside
with their tails stuck up in the air
who they thought were their friends.

Nuage Argente

Nuage Argente –
the name of the house
you betrayed us in,
sucking each other to bits
like two chunks of chopped fish
made fat from feeding on the blood and tears
of other people's partners
and your own.
What a noise
you must be making
behind the curtains
in the little room.
You sometimes soak the sheets.
You sometimes lie.
You 'can't believe you did this'.
Nor can I.
Every day I'll dip you in my syrup.
I'll dip you in and force you to be lovable
and roll you around
in trays of hundreds and thousands.
The lowest of the low my mother called them,
men who messed with other people's wives.
Today's today.
It will not come again.
Somewhere in your heart
there must be tenderness.
If you've got one.
Which they say you have.
You know how farmers
run their hands through grain
to coax large animals to come to them?
I'm running my words
through buckets of prayers like that
to coax something out of the dark
to come and save us.

My Happiest Day

My happiest day was not my wedding day.
My happiest day
was the day we all played baseball
after exams were over
out on the baseball pitch,
I had been lying all night
with encyclopaedias piled on top of me
'to strengthen my limbs'
and I had come out onto the pitch
in the immaculate Jerusalem-white clothes
I had spent all morning
cleaning and pressing and peeling on and off,
and when the ball came sailing out of the clouds
towards my hands
I was the one who caught it –
my hands,
like laps,
or home,
barely touching its belly
as I guided it out of the sky.
Mother Maria yelled *Catch*
and I caught it every time.
So what's so great about catching a baseball ball?
What's the use of being so happy then?
I've got to concentrate on catching everything
you and the world and its wives
and various pungent mistresses
care to throw at me now,
aged fifty-one.
And Mother Maria's got nothing to do with it.
She probably never even touched a man.

My Private Sky

My mother hung her washing in the clouds
high among the buzzards and the rocks.
My washing-line today is the same.
It sails through the sky like a ship
unknown to men. Men never come this far,
only their obedient large clothes,
only me, my mother and her hens,
only buzzards, only wind and rain –
until the day she suddenly appeared,
dropped her luggage on my flower-beds,
and hung her washing in my private sky.

Ice

Can't she see she's blocking out my light,
can't she see that everything she does
is blocking out my light
like little kings
I duck and duck and feel exhausted by
that smell of her
and make me so uptight
I'd rather be a wall than a wife
and then I would not have to hear the plop
of ice-cubes in her double gin?
Forget it.
'The little things.'
Her little scarf.
Forget it.
She smiles and says she likes my dog.
Forget it.

My Wedding Ring

I hammered it out like a palette-knife,
flat, for a minnow,
(you wouldn't get that)
or a shrunken platinum plaque
with your love message still engraved on it
in barely-visible loops
as if the dried bodies of sea-horses
had journeyed from a sea
you couldn't even look at without swimming in
it was so blue –
and now you say you don't know what I mean.
I'm not surprised after last night.
I've never been so close to another woman,
a woman brimming over with the details
my 'real' friends were kind enough to spare me,
brimming over like the sandwich box
of maddened wasps
you left on the cooker that night
till the plastic started to melt
and stick to their wings,
and I scraped the whole singed tangle into the sink,
and some of them were trying to clamber out –
and I'm trying not to post you back your ring,
make a little parcel of it for you,
tissue-paper, bows, a little note.
But what's the use? You wouldn't understand.
I might just as well post you
this sudden undignified craving
for tinned milk
I keep giving in to, and sucking,
like *Who shall I cling to,*
who shall I cling to now?

Her Little Turquoise Scarf

When I found her little turquoise scarf
I got a pair of scissors from the drawer,
split her little turquoise jungles open
and sent her parrots screeching to the door.

Green Glass Arms

I wanted them to lock you in a palace;
I wanted dogs to find you there years later
with eggs she has thrown at you
caked all over your face
and doors smashed open
and lights ripped out of their sockets
and all that billing and cooing
that made you sound like unrepentant turtle-doves
with fire-engines embedded in your throats
you couldn't stop
now stopped for good;
I wanted you to get
so sick of one another
she'd tear you to bits in a rage
and leave the country –
but what I've done's invent myself a parrot,
a very persistent parrot
that has got it into his head
that I have to be taught parrot language,
and all the time that he's trotting along beside me
looking exotic,
or hanging upside-down like someone practising
how not to handle an egg,
he's telling me in no uncertain terms
his mother was a lettuce-coloured ostrich
as round and satisfactory as the moon,
and *yes*, he squawks, he wants to live with me,
and tell me lies, and eat my nuts and oranges;
and in the evenings,
when the sun has set,
engulf me in his wicked green glass arms.

The Man I Never Married

I wrote and told his mother we were married.
What a lie. He never even touched me.
I told her out of kindness, I suppose.
And out of kindness sent a photograph
not of him but of a tennis star
to prop beside her bed above the optician's
she lay and waited for his letters in,
dressed in a fox-fur coat and a pair of spectacles
that scraped against her pillow like a crab.
And when she heard the news,
and saw the photograph,
she dragged her leaking body from the bed –
or would have done if Nurse hadn't held her down.
And very soon, attended by the tennis star,
and wrapped in baby foxes,
she was dead.

A Day in the Life of Your Suitcase

The sun is shining brightly when your suitcase
steps, a little stiffly, from its bed
and hurries down the road to the beach
where suitcases of every description
are leaping up and down in the air
looking like a flock of battered monuments
or bits of bedroom learning how to fly.
And look at yours. It used to be your wife.
Now it's half a suitcase, half a bird,
trying to get its lid to be its wing.
And as it lunges off towards the sunset
it's hawking up a load of old dresses
and sausages and clocks and double-beds
that fan across the heavens like a jumble-sale,
plunging the whole country into darkness.

I Know I Ought to Love You

I know I ought to love you
but it's hopeless.
Screaming is the best I can do.
I scream at you for such a long time
that even when I stop the scream goes on.
It screams between us like a frozen street
with stiff exhausted birds embedded in it.

Being Single

Being single's never being nude.
Being single's wearing hats in bed.
Being single's trying to get to sleep
and constantly being interrupted
by important-looking spiders
marching off
to the best poison shops;
by moths like bats
banging their fat heads
against my pillow;
by bats whose plan
is to station themselves in my hair,
by mean-looking flies
doing their lengths on my window,
and indomitable old cockchafers
rehearsing their clicketty-clacks
at such a pitch
all I want to do is go to sleep
and dream about a woman – is it me? –
running towards you with her arms outstretched
in a little knee-length dress that suits her perfectly.
But no. I can't.
I've got to stay awake.
Every ant in England's on its way.
They're coming in red columns from all sides
driving flocks of ferocious-looking sheep.

The Man Who Said He Had
Danced with Twyla Tharp

I'd like to own a shop selling shoes.
Only men's, only certain men's, and only shoes.
I won't be needing men –
the fish on legs
that other people sleep with,
slipping in and out of rippling sheets
accompanied by blunt and jellied bodies
forever searching for an inland sea
they've never been to
yet are homesick for
somewhere in the West beyond wild plateaux
white with driven lilies and warm snow.
I don't know what they do there
when they get there.
Maybe there's a boat,
a small hotel.
Maybe there's a rippling double-bed
on which to start
all over again.
Anyway I've never been that far.
Maybe close. In 1968.
With a man who said he had danced with Twyla Tharp.
OK he was small.
It doesn't matter.
Everyone is on the same side.
What side is that?
Of wanting to be good.
Every day I tell myself *Remember:*
somewhere in your heart
there must be tenderness.
What we've got to do is try and find it.
What we've got to do is find it soon.

Being Angry

How can I reach the small clean rooms
of the former hospital where bees fly in and out
of flowers as big as drawing-rooms
and the lake's so close
you can fish in its lap from your bed
and the residents ask you for nothing,
if asking for love is for nothing,
and even the sand on the shore
is seamlessly gold,
if I won't stand up?
Nothing works.
Nothing makes me move.
I lie here with my eyes all clouded over
and insects sucking
where my legs should be –
and as I speak they're pouring up my arms
and crawling down my throat
as if they own me.

The Visitations of Prejudiced Angels

The luxuriant ears of someone I won't mention,
who sleeps as if he's only just been born,
as if he hasn't learnt how not to sleep
or where to lay his sleepy head down yet,
the luxuriant golden hair,
that sticks up on top of his head like a pet field
giving him the contented unmarried look
of somebody establishing
a small picnic area on their head,
complete with bees,
of somebody who's trained a pair of sloths
to sing to them before they go to bed,
fill my nights
like the visitations of prejudiced angels
all breathlessly susurrating around me
to block her out.

Chocolate Sardines

They tell me to be tough: *be tough*, they say.
Be tough yourself.
I refuse to be.
His favourite food awaits him in the fridge –
his favourite fish,
like his mother bought him –
their silver eyes and eyeball-coloured scales
keeping cool inside its frosty door
like slivers of bright nights
when we were lovers.
Take that back.
Lovers sounds ridiculous.
Nights when everyone else
but us
were lovers.

The World's Entire Wasp Population

This feeling I can't get rid of,
this feeling that someone's been reading
my secret diary
that I kept in our bedroom
because I thought nobody else but us
would want to go in there,
except it's not my diary,
it's my husband,
I'd like you to smear this feeling
all over and into her naked body like jam
and invite the world's entire wasp population,
the sick, the halt, the fuzzy,
to enjoy her.

The Smell of the Women

The smell of the women
you drove all over the country
like pet princesses,
the smell of their bags,
the smell of their leopard-skin-gift-wrapped
powders and creams
from pink boutiques in caffeinated cities
drove me away;
and now I'm here, with me,
where sheets can be as spotless as they please,
and roads are white, unhurried, leading nowhere,
and men are turned to chickens at the border,
except for those like you I turn to marble
to think things over for a million years.

Your Thumbs

Your thumbs, your back, your car,
your girlfriend's car,
like the gristly rocks
banging and rumbling in boiling water
beneath the buried sand-dunes of Siberia,
are what I think of
when I think of you;
but what I want to think of is the man
I want to still be fond of when it's over.

Your Face

I haven't seen your face for so long now
I feel like a small exhausted traveller
who, coming home one evening in late summer
across familiar fields in fine rain,
finds a ruin where her house should be
and no one there to greet her at the gate.

Her Little Turquoise Dress

When I saw her,
when I actually saw her
standing in her little turquoise dress
so close to me
I could have almost licked her,
far from seeing lips
encased in hailstones
containing the splintery bones
of deep-frozen kingfishers,
what I saw was a tiny blue woman
swimming around inside a drop of gin.
And at that moment, by her side, I loved her.
At precisely six o'clock
I *definitely loved her.*
I felt it as an unfamiliar arching,
or stretching, of the roof of my mouth.

Her Turquoise Breasts

It's time to say goodbye to your wife.
It's time to chuck me out and say goodbye
and let your mind contain only water
for someone I'm the predecessor of
to float around in in her turquoise bra,
its turquoise cups uplifting turquoise breasts
you obviously can't wait
to make the most of.

The Little Dog

If all the glassy skyscrapers of Chicago
were crushed together in a solid lump
and chilled for a million years
and given legs
and set to walk alone
along our streets,
it would not be as icy cold as you
whose heart is frozen like a little dog
that's lost its way far out on the snow,
and people searched –
it was a much-loved dog –
but long ago gave up
and turned for home.

Painting the Summer-house

I've suddenly realised
I can't remember your face,
or if I do it's only the lips I remember
reduced by a life-time of panic
to razor-blades
I'm happily turning into apricots
I can almost touch already
from my step-ladder.

I Want a Lover

I said *I want a lover*. It's not true.
I'm happy as I am being happy
pretending I'm a large kangaroo.
The males are red – not my favourite colour –
and spend their time boxing one another.
The females are lazier, and lovelier –
our bodies are a misty violet-blue,
and filled with sand, and given useful elbows,
and told to spend the day doing nothing
but munching grass and watching parakeets;
and if we meet a wife, to be encouraging,
and tell her what she hopes is out here is.

Your Blue Shirt

I wonder if you ever still wear it,
and if you think of me when you do,
or are your clothes completely different now,
and does she choose them for you, does she take you
and dress you in fine suits of spun camellias
and ties of intricately-woven ostrich feathers,
do you sleep in sheets of sliced champagne
on beds of solid diamond sprayed with stars?
And why get so upset about a shirt?
Because it made your body feel warm.
It made your body feel like a stone
I like to think I warmed my cheek against.

Following Stars

Following stars and maps
that make perfect sense
or if they don't
it doesn't seem to matter,
roaming the world
with my cargo of notebooks and tea,
with my good-looking parrots and babies,
my good-looking shoes,
I am myself again;
and as for you,
you're better off without me definitely.

Being a Grandmother

First, there is a smell of custard-cremes
baking in a custard-creme factory.
And mixed with that you smell a hint of gorse,
of roasted pods cracking on hot cliffs.
Inhale again, and what you smell is stars.
It smells so sweet you smell a little more.
Be careful though. The scent has strange effects:
everything goes quiet. You stay indoors.
You wash your hands. You smile. You lose your way.
At night you meet small animals in bonnets.
You turn a sort of misty violet grey,
and start to sing. And never stop singing.
Men walk past with buckets on their heads.
Some of them, alas, no longer know you.

Your New Shoes

To her, this must be you being you.
To me, you're like a man who's been undressed
and wheeled away to some remote annexe
where women in white skirts and rubber gloves
plump you up and rouge you like a corpse
then wheel you back into the world again,
complete with hair and teeth and new shoes.

No one Else

When I think of you I think of you
and no one else,
and nothing else matters,
it's warm outside,
I'm giving birth to ducks,
they waddle off,
adorable, ridiculous,
to eat their meals standing on their heads,
then waddle back,
my homing eiderdowns,
to use my new-found mercy for their bed.

House of Cows

Yes, you are invited to a ball
to which not only you
but our solicitors,
our counsellors, plumbers, gynaecologists,
station-masters, fishmongers and bank-managers
are warmly, are lovingly, invited;
and it won't matter in the least to anyone
that all the coloured sandwiches
are falling to bits
and a woman in an Alsatian-coloured dress
is handing round a tray of rotten tomatoes
and guests just stand and stare like blocks of fish,
because we are about to spend the night
dancing like we've never danced before,
dancing till the sun lights up the sky
and anger is no more than some old clock
ringing to itself in ancient ruins
only the occasional large cow
wanders in and out of
munching flowers.

Mr and Mrs Cosy

They stayed with us for twenty-five years —
cooked and cleaned
and never said a thing.
People thought they wanted to be there,
and so did we,
and so, in fact, did they —
until the day they realised their mistake,
and shook their little fists,
and looked so glum
we packed their bags
and sent them on their way
to somewhere warm and cosy, with good food,
where, sinking into matching leather sofas,
the two of them need never work again.

The Man Who Looks for Waterfalls

The little man who looks for waterfalls,
whose ears are long,
whose hands are small and icy,
who's here one minute gone the next like light;
who hides himself in passage-ways
in hillsides
to offer up his face
to wandering snails,
wants to be alone with me. I know that.
To lie beside me in the dead of night
like ash out late shifting its pink fur
on beds of rock we'll watch the moon rise from –
deafened
by the elongated lake
that doesn't know what else to do
but fall.

When He Follows Me into the Café Looking Nervous

When he follows me like this, I want to say —
when he follows me into the café
looking as nervous and excited
as somebody following a river
in search of waterfalls
to slip inside his coat
before they fly out
into the ballrooms of the night
like wild horses
galloping across the sky
with chariots full of fishes
at their heels
dressed in skin-tight
crunchy sequined dresses
that can't stop dancing
faster and faster like Catherine Wheels
for fear of collapsing
down on their knees till they crack
and whisper *do it do it* —
don't be shy.

The Slinky Dress

I would never have written the letter
without the dress
that seems to release me into a kind of heaven
by far the most radiant angel in is me,
darkened only by the large shadows

his hands that track my dress like hunters cast
till I no longer know if it is him,
the slinky dress,
or love itself I love.
Love itself, surprisingly, feels cold.

So if he wants to sleep with me tonight
let him be a tiny naked fish –
or a tiny fish in a T-shirt if he must –
and swim inside my lake of liquid ice
shop assistants kindly sell in TOPSHOP.

The Waterfall Man

I keep them in white lofts like tall pigeons
and train their long brown arms to carry messages
to somebody I know who will have walked
beside the river like the river's groom
for so long now his body will be brown,
boneless, supple, tipped with eyes like sprays
and muscular as otters dipped in glass.
His famous leather boots will creak like ice.
His tongue will have the grace and strength of syrup.

Because of him, because of his bright eyes,
his crunchy fish-and-gravel-coloured boots;
because of water pouring through my nights
with a sound like an endless supply
of crystal-glass sewing-machines
cascading through the sky
still systematically machining the seams
of a thousand taffeta dresses
encrusted with jewels and zips and tight bodices;

because he's half a man and half a waterfall
there's no such thing as sleeping any more.
To other people,
he's the Head Librarian.
He stands behind his desk and looks severe.
To me,
he'll always be the small man
who roams the world in search of waterfalls,
a woman's eye-lids tucked behind his ear.

I Will Be Arriving Next Thursday
in My Wedding-Dress

I will be arriving next Thursday in my wedding-dress.
I will be arriving next Thursday morning
at seven o'clock
in a white satin wedding-dress
the colour and texture
of one-hundred-per-cent-fit Bull Terriers
that feel like eels;
he will hear me
calling his name across the waterfalls,
and, craning his neck
(he's as small as a small jockey),
he will suddenly see me
staring at him through his kitchen window –
my ankle-length satin wedding-dress
dragged over to one side by a large rucksack
containing nougat, maps
and a rocky island
crossed by the tracks of relays of stocky horses
carrying the world's fiercest
and most nimble seamstresses
towards a bed piled high for him and me
with eiderdowns that hold a million lips
peeled from the heads of skilfully-dried
small lovers.